T0207921

THE AFRICAN-AMERICAN
COMMUNITY
AND ITS NEED FOR VENTURE CAPITAL

JASON M. FIELDS

authorHOUSE®

AuthorHouse™
1663 Liberty Drive
Bloomington, IN 47403
www.authorhouse.com
Phone: 1 (800) 839-8640

Published by AuthorHouse 10/12/2018

ISBN: 978-1-5462-6424-8 (sc)
ISBN: 978-1-5462-6422-4 (hc)
ISBN: 978-1-5462-6423-1 (e)

Library of Congress Control Number: 2018912257

Print information available on the last page.

This book is printed on acid-free paper.

NOTES TO THE READER

While the author of this book have made reasonable efforts to ensure the accuracy and timeliness of the information contained herein, the author and publisher assume no liability with respect to loss or damage caused, or alleged to be caused, by any reliance on any information contained herein and disclaim any and all warranties, expressed or implied, as to the accuracy or reliability of said information. The authors make no representations or warranties with respect to the accuracy or completeness of the contents of this work and specifically disclaim all warranties. The advice and strategies contained herein may not be suitable for every situation. It is the complete responsibility of the reader to ensure they are adhering to all local, regional and national laws. This publication is designed to provide accurate and authoritative information in regard to the subject matter covered.

INTRODUCTION

Many of us as investors spend every waking hour calculating the present deal, worrying about the last deal, and dreaming of the next. Our nights are spent fighting the constrictive entanglement of our bed sheets as we roll endlessly, fighting to find solutions to the problems of our daily lives. We are subjected to the constant chaos of our compulsive thinking, with never even a moment's peace. The noise making activity of our thoughts is our constant companion, ever so repetitive, unceasing, circular, and unproductive. But what happened to us? It didn't used to be this way. Why is everything so stressful, uneven, chaotic, dramatic, and generally in the opposite direction of what we see as progress? The answer is not where you might think it is.

The answer lies in the fact that "time" as we know it is actually an illusion. There is really no past or no future. All that exists is the NOW. This moment, this second, this instant, is all we really have to work with, as the past is dead and gone, and the future is just a fantasy.

The root of our problem is in the concept that something in the future, some acquisition, some amount of money will make us whole and complete, and it is at this future moment we will be happy. We can't be happy now as we are lacking. Only the future holds our satisfaction. This concept turns us into the forever lacking "human doing" rather than the "human being" that we actually are. We have no peace due to the fact that only a future idea holds the key to happiness. Just like the race track dogs chasing the Styrofoam rabbit, we can never catch what we "lack". But all of this is just an illusion, spawned from our past experience, our present knowledge, and our mental conceptual boundaries of what we see as possible and impossible.

Where can we possibly find the answer to this paradox? Should we go to a high mountain alone to meditate on the question "what is truth"?". Do we cast off our worldly possessions and go on a quest to find the paradoxical "sourceless source". What about the expression "a caught fish is a dead fish" relating to the capture and isolation of truth?

All of these ideas are indeed as absurd as they are close to the essence of the truth. The real point we must capture, is that we are already complete and whole right now. Nothing in the future will bring us any closer to our perfection than the ever present Now. The truth actually lies right were we are standing! The strength of our will comes from the realization that true security lies not in what we have, but what we can do without. If we can identify this truth, then this truth can liberate.

The concept of true joy coming from the actual point on which we are standing may seem odd at first glance, but try the concept on for just a moment. We truly are "living the life" as we have the freedom that entrepreneurship gives us. We have the capacity to learn and the intellect to step beyond the mentality of the W2 wage slave to spread our wings and fly. The truth is that we all have this capacity for joy, the creative ability, and the purity of heart. We actually have the capacity to enjoy ever minute of everyday if we believe it's possible. Therein lies to key!

There exists 4 levels of activity in our lives. The first level of activity gives us such joy and satisfaction in a way that the more we do it the more we love it. The results we produce are always outstanding. Second level are activities that we do with great ease and superior results, but we don't feel the magnetic pull to spend more time doing it. The third level are the joyless activities that we can accomplish, and produce mediocre results. These activities drain us of excitement, ambition and happiness. Finally, the fourth level are activities that we hate, produce terrible results, and avoid at all costs. The problem lies in the way we divide our time among these different levels, not the activities themselves.

The truth of happiness lies in doing ONLY the level one activities, and delegating the other activities to those who can do them better. The penny wise and dollar foolish investors spends time in these chores "saving money" but at a costly burdening his or her spirit. We are all truly able to be a Donald Trump, Mother Teresa, Shakespeare, or Socrates if we can recognize our true purpose. How do you do that? It lies within the level one activities, if we can listen. The way we feel will guide us to our true purpose. Just pay attention to what you are feeling as you going through your daily routine. Is there joy and happiness in what I am doing at this moment? Do I feel a sense of peace and clarity of thought when I am engaged in what I am doing? If you feel this, you are on the right pathway. If not, either change what you are doing, delegate it, or stop! Realize the truth is you have complete control over this, and your happiness, and peace is inside of you right now.

CHAPTER ONE

THE LACK OF ACCESS TO CAPITAL IN OUR COMMUNITIES

(THE PROBLEM)

Throughout America, minority communities are being undermined by a problem that may, in some ways, be as pernicious as underfunded schools, inadequate housing, and a scarcity of public amenities like parks and libraries. It is a problem, moreover, that goes largely unnoticed and that is not fully understood, save for a few who are steeped in the issue or grapple with it daily. The problem—inadequate capital access for minority-owned businesses—is depriving minority communities of their own source of wealth and jobs.

Capital is the heart of businesses. Businesses, in turn, are the economic pillars of our communities, providing secure jobs and the opportunity to generate the kind of wealth that can be passed down through generations. Forty percent of the net new jobs created in the past two decades were the result of hiring by new businesses. For communities that suffer from high rates of unemployment and joblessness, minority-owned firms are economic life preservers, bringing a strong tax base and economic opportunity into these underserved communities.

A lack of capital access has ramifications beyond minority communities. Consider this: if the minority business community had reached economic parity in 2002, the Minority Business Development Agency (MBDA) estimates that "the minority business community would have employed more than 16 million workers, generated more than $2.5 trillion in gross receipts, and expanded the tax base by more than $100 billion."

Lack of capital is one of the primary reasons that small businesses flounder. For new businesses, working capital bridges the gap to keep operations running smoothly and the bills paid on time. For established businesses, capital is a lifeline for expansion, allowing businesses to hire new employees, open new stores, and upgrade technology and equipment.

Access to capital is even more critical in the technology sector. Here, the impact of early-stage financing on success is tremendous. Receiving a loan increases survival probability by 51 percent, according to researchers. Yet minority owned firms continue to be less likely than non-minority owned businesses to receive the funding they need.

When minority-owned firms do receive loans, the dollar value is often less, while the interest rates tend to be higher, according to research from the Minority Business Development Agency. The average loan amount for minority-owned businesses with gross receipts over $500,000 is $149,000, compared with $310,000 for their non-minority owned counterparts.

The United States has a long, enviable entrepreneurial culture. If we are to continue as a world leader in innovation, we must foster broad participation in economic growth. This starts with removing barriers to capital expansion and empowering more entrepreneurs with the skills and resources they need to succeed. We must develop strategies and policy recommendations for achieving economic parity. And we must strengthen partnerships across the government, business and financial services sectors.

Now is the time to advance America's promise of opportunity, prosperity, and growth for all.

We believe that while pattern recognition has enabled investors to mitigate risk, it has also limited their profit potential

Jason M. Fields is the Managing Director at Dark Night Capital Ventures, LLC a organization dedicated to advancing the global black community by developing VC Funding opportunities.

Our venture fund/company has a unique value proposition and it will be beneficial to you. By investing in underrepresented communities, minorities, women, veterans, etc..can generate positive returns on your investments, and it is also a good idea both economically and socially.

CHAPTER TWO

HOW PATTERN RECOGNITION HURTS AMERICA

(LACK OF DIVERSITY OF ENTREPRENEURS)

Why diversification is a big challenge for business owners

Business owners' greatest strengths are often their greatest weaknesses as well. The determination, willingness to take risks and relentless pursuit of a goal may be desirable characteristics for building a business, but not necessarily suited to sound investment planning.

Inevitably, business owners must take risks when they launch their companies. They may have sacrificed a secure income and taken on responsibility for both their own investment in the company and the wealth of others who have entrusted them with money as loans or investment. They are facing tough odds – while estimates vary, around 80% of new businesses fail within 18 months – and they usually have to surmount significant obstacles.

The qualities required make for great entrepreneurs, but may not be ideal for taking a balanced view of wealth planning. First is the focus on a single goal. Business owners tend to hold their wealth in just one or two assets – usually their business and their home(s). From one perspective, this makes sense. Why devote your life to your business if you're not willing to 'eat your own lunch'? Business owners often believe they can achieve a far better return on investment than any wealth manager.

Business owners may also be over-confident – after all, entrepreneurs defy the odds to build a business. This can lead them to underestimate risk and fail to see the value in diversification, whether in their business or in their portfolio of investments and assets.

These are valuable instincts without which entrepreneurs would be less successful in their primary activity, but it can be worth taking other steps to protect both the business and the owner's personal wealth. Part of this is just down to common sense. Businesses are always at the mercy of market conditions. Sectors can be cyclical, and even the strongest business may find itself subject to forces beyond its control, from central bank interest rate policy to disruptive technological innovation.

There are also liquidity considerations. A company owner that needs money at short notice cannot always sell a portion of the business rapidly. Bringing in new sources of funding takes time. It makes sense to have alternative options available through personal wealth planning to ensure that the business isn't liable to be compromised by personal financial considerations.

Lifestyle will also play a role. Company owners who have worked extremely long hours over several decades to build a sustainable business may feel that they want to start enjoying some of the wealth they have created. This will prompt a shift in focus from wealth creation to wealth preservation, which may necessitate a change in financial planning strategy.

Diversifying a business

A key aspect of protecting entrepreneurial wealth is found in good business practice. While many entrepreneurs may be seduced, to some extent, by the prospect of a multi-million-euro sale of their start-up to a big group with deep pockets, in reality this type of speedy realisation of the business's value is rare, and usually requires a remarkable proprietary technological innovation, or ideal timing. Even with a thriving business, exiting is unlikely to be this easy. To survive, businesses have to be built to last, rather than for short-term gains.

Building for the long term rather than that elusive rapid flip calls for diversity of clients, of revenues and of funding, all vital to longer-term survival and growth. For example, many owners keep ploughing their own capital or those of friends and family into their business.

Often entrepreneurs are highly resistant to ceding any kind of control to external shareholders or funding providers, but bringing in alternative funding can be an important discipline for businesses, as well as the added benefit of an injection of new ideas. It can also be important if one funding source dries up for some reason – weak cash flow is usually the fatal blow for smaller enterprises.

Similarly, aiming to have as broad as possible a diversity of clients, and therefore of revenues, should be sound business practice. This is not always possible, but it should be a consistent ambition.

Developing a diversification plan

While the exact mix of cash, bonds, stock market investments, real estate and other assets may be different for every entrepreneur and depend on individual circumstances, age, preferences and risk tolerance, the starting point for diversification is the same. If the business ran into a major financial problem – an economic recession, a natural disaster such as fire or flood, or an illness keeping the owner from work for an extended period of time – could their business and personal finances stay afloat?

If the business is a high-risk asset, dependent on economic conditions and tying up the bulk of an individual's wealth, they should not be taking similar risks elsewhere – the portfolio should be balanced with lower-risk assets that are less vulnerable to the economic climate.

A diversification plan requires analysis of everything from an individual's spending habits and family commitments to retirement provision. The solution will often need to comprise not just investments but insurance, such as key man risk and illness cover.

The asset mix for entrepreneurs may well not be the same as for other investors. They must consider the business, as it is in many cases the owner's largest asset. They should consider the prospect of a future sale or all or part of the company, which can influence tax, succession and inheritance planning.

While having all their eggs in one basket, as entrepreneurs tend to do, can be highly motivating, it can be extremely painful when things go wrong. Taking steps to diversify can ensure that entrepreneurs have a solid foundation to fall back on during difficult times

Where venture capitalists invest and why

Entrepreneurs looking to raise capital are often told that investors like to keep things close to home. Is that true? The question influences where people locate companies. After all, if investors are only willing to invest in their own backyard, you might be better off starting your next company as close to capital as possible. Unless, of course, the conventional wisdom is wrong and investors are more flexible than we might have thought.

The argument in favor of investing locally is simple: Face-to-face meetings are much easier to facilitate when everyone's within a short car ride or public transit trip from one another. Even in a time where video chatting is near-ubiquitous, there's still something to be said for convening in person. Again, it makes sense.

"So what," you might be asking yourself. Isn't it obvious that investors would rather invest close to home, when possible? Sure, but as is typically the case with most plainly obvious things, when one takes a slightly closer look, nuance and variation abound.

How Venture Capital Works

As noted above, small firms lack access to the capital markets. And they are often too new or too small to get traditional bank loans. The businesses often start out by using capital provided by the business owners. But as is often the case with startup businesses, profitability is a few years in coming. So once the owners have tapped their own financial resources, they have to look for outside sources of financing in order to grow the business.

The business principals will often seek out either a venture capital firm or an angel investor (see description of angel investors below) to provide funding for this purpose.

The business submits a business plan to the venture capital firm. The venture capital firm will then investigate the business. This will include a full investigation and analysis of the company's business model, products, financial position and performance, the history of the principals of the business, the industry it's engaged in and many other factors.

If the venture capital firm decides to go ahead and invest in the startup, they will make a proposal. That will include the amount of the investment that they are willing to make. The firm will also specify the equity stake in the company that they expect to have in return. That investment of VC money typically takes place in phases, commonly referred to as rounds. There may be several rounds of funding taking place over several years.

Funding Rounds

The funding will be provided in rounds in part because the venture capitalist wants to be sure that the startup is meeting its expected goals and projections. In fact, each subsequent round of financing may be dependent upon the company meeting a succession of goals. The venture capital firm may even take an active role in managing the company's business. That involvement is often an advantage to the startup, since venture capitalists have extensive experience in growing companies.

The venture capitalist will expect to be invested in the startup for several years, giving the company a chance to grow and meet its expected goals. The payoff comes when the startup is either acquired by another company or launches its initial public offering (IPO).

In either case, the acquisition or IPO is expected to produce a substantial rate of return on the amount of money invested by the venture capital firm.

Why Would an Investor Invest in Venture Capital?

VC funding is undoubtedly one of the highest risk types of investing there is. This is because the risk of failure by startup companies is greater than the likelihood of success. In fact, more than 70% of startups fail at some point in the VC process.

It may be that the company's business model fails or that it runs into heavier than expected competition. It may also fail because it is unable to raise follow-on funding (subsequent rounds of additional financing). Many startups are funded by multiple venture capital firms. So there's always the chance that one or more could decide not to continue at some point during the startup process.

But despite those risks, VC funding can be incredibly profitable. For example, a venture capitalist might invest $20 million in a startup in exchange for a 20% equity position in the company. If the startup raises $1 billion in its IPO, the venture capitalist equity stake will rise to $200 million. That will give them a 10 to 1 return on their initial investment.

Given that so many business startups fail, venture capital firms invest in multiple startups on a continuous basis. It's understood that some will fail but that enough will succeed — and succeed spectacularly — to offset the losses and to produce substantial returns. For example, a single 10 to 1 profit on a successful VC deal could easily offset losses on five failed startups.

Sources of Venture Capital

A venture capitalist could be a wealthy individual, or it may be a venture capital firm that is comprised of multiple wealthy individuals. In addition, investment banks and other financial institutions get involved in VC funding, often forming partnerships.

Since the investors are wealthy, they can afford to take the kinds of losses that come with VC funding. But they are usually the type of investors who are looking for much higher returns on their money than will be available with traditional investments like bank investments, bonds, stocks, mutual funds and exchange traded funds.

VC investing offers a much higher potential return on their money. Such investors usually have the kind of wealth where they can have most of their money in lower risk traditional investments, while devoting a small percentage of their portfolios to high risk VC lending in the pursuit of much higher returns.

Venture capital firms can also be highly specialized. Taking advantage of the expertise gained in certain industries or perhaps those where the firm has enjoyed a particularly high level of success, a VC firm might concentrate in either a small number of industries or even a single industry. For example, a VC firm might specialize in technology upstarts. Many VC firms will also bring industry expertise to the deal. So they can provide a non-financial benefit to the startup company.

You can find venture capital firms through the National Venture Capital Association (NVCA). This is an organization that represents hundreds of VC firms.

How You Can Invest Like a Venture Capitalist

In recent years, the internet has made investment platforms possible that let you invest like a venture capitalist. These sites let investors take advantage of unprecedented deals — especially through crowdfunding.

These sites allow small businesses and entrepreneurs to secure funds from a pool of small, individual investors. That way, they don't have to pitch an idea to one big venture capital firm. Dozens or even hundreds of investors may fund a single offering.

The investors themselves will have the opportunity to invest in deals that might not have been available to them otherwise. And some of these opportunities have the potential to be huge.

Here's at **https://www.darkknightcapital.com** one of the coolest platforms out there that let you act like a venture capitalist, we have what it takes to invest.

CHAPTER THREE

WE NEED INVESTORS NOT LOANS!

(VENTURE CAPITAL VS LOANS, THE DIFFERENCE IS?)

Business owners with poor or non-existent credit may have a more difficult time obtaining a business loan.

Venture Capital

Venture Capital investors will provide significant sums of money for a stake in the company. A typical venture capitalist may require a portion of the profits, a position on the board or a certain number of shares within the company before providing financial backing. However, you get a lot in return, least of all access to their network of industry contacts.

Venture capital is money provided by professionals who invest alongside management in young, rapidly growing companies that have the potential to develop into significant economic contributors. Venture capital is an important source of equity for start-up companies.

Professionally managed venture capital firms generally are private partnerships or closely-held corporations funded by private and public pension funds, endowment funds, foundations, corporations, wealthy individuals, foreign investors, and the venture capitalists themselves.

Venture capitalists generally:

- Finance new and rapidly growing companies;
- Purchase equity securities;
- Assist in the development of new products or services;
- Add value to the company through active participation;
- Take higher risks with the expectation of higher rewards;
- Have a long-term orientation for

When considering an investment, venture capitalists carefully screen the technical and business merits of the proposed company. Venture capitalists only invest in a small percentage of the businesses they review and have a long-term perspective. Going forward, they actively work with the company's management by contributing their experience and business savvy gained from helping other companies with similar growth challenges.

Venture capitalists mitigate the risk of venture investing by developing a portfolio of young companies in a single venture fund. Many times they will co-invest with other professional venture capital firms. In addition, many venture partnership will manage multiple funds simultaneously. For decades, venture capitalists have nurtured the growth of America's high technology and entrepreneurial communities resulting in significant job creation, economic growth and international competitiveness. Companies such as Digital Equipment Corporation, Apple, Federal Express, Compaq, Sun Microsystems, Intel, Microsoft and Genentech are famous examples of companies that received venture capital early in their development.

Private Equity Investing

Venture capital investing has grown from a small investment pool in the 1960s and early 1970s to a mainstream asset class that is a viable and significant part of the institutional and corporate investment portfolio. Recently, some investors have been referring to venture investing and buyout investing as "private equity investing." This term can be confusing because some in the investment industry use the term "private equity" to refer only to buyout fund investing.

In any case, an institutional investor will allocate 2% to 3% of their institutional portfolio for investment in alternative assets such as private equity or venture capital as part of their overall asset allocation. Currently, over 50% of investments in venture capital/private equity comes from institutional public and private pension funds, with the balance coming from endowments, foundations, insurance companies, banks, individuals and other entities who seek to diversify their portfolio with this investment class.

What is a Venture Capitalist?

The typical person-on-the-street depiction of a venture capitalist is that of a wealthy financier who wants to fund start-up companies. The perception is that a person who develops a brand new change-the-world invention needs capital; thus, if they can't get capital from a bank or from their own pockets, they enlist the help of a venture capitalist.

In truth, venture capital and private equity firms are pools of capital, typically organized as a limited partnership, that invests in companies that represent the opportunity for a high rate of return within five to seven years. The venture capitalist may look at several hundred investment opportunities before investing in only a few selected companies with favorable investment opportunities. Far from being simply passive financiers, venture capitalists foster growth in companies through their involvement in the management, strategic marketing and planning of their investee companies. They are entrepreneurs first and financiers second.

Even individuals may be venture capitalists. In the early days of venture capital investment, in the 1950s and 1960s, individual investors were the archetypal venture investor. While this type of individual investment did not totally disappear, the modern venture firm emerged as the dominant venture investment vehicle. However, in the last few years, individuals have again become a potent and increasingly larger part of the early stage start-up venture life cycle. These "angel investors" will mentor a company and provide needed capital and expertise to help develop companies. Angel investors may either be wealthy people with management expertise or retired business men and women who seek the opportunity for first-hand business development.

Investment Focus

Venture capitalists may be generalist or specialist investors depending on their investment strategy. Venture capitalists can be generalists, investing in various industry sectors, or various geographic locations, or various stages of a company's life. Alternatively, they may be specialists in one or two industry sectors, or may seek to invest in only a localized geographic area.

Not all venture capitalists invest in "start-ups." While venture firms will invest in companies that are in their initial start-up modes, venture capitalists will also invest in companies at various stages of the business life cycle. A venture capitalist may invest before there is a real product or company organized (so called "seed investing"), or may provide capital to start up a company in its first or second stages of development known as "early stage investing." Also, the venture capitalist may provide needed financing to help a company grow beyond a critical mass to become more successful ("expansion stage financing").

The venture capitalist may invest in a company throughout the company's life cycle and therefore some funds focus on later stage investing by providing financing to help the company grow to a critical mass to attract public financing through a stock offering. Alternatively, the venture capitalist may help the company attract a merger or acquisition with another company by providing liquidity and exit for the company's founders.

At the other end of the spectrum, some venture funds specialize in the acquisition, turnaround or recapitalization of public and private companies that represent favorable investment opportunities.

There are venture funds that will be broadly diversified and will invest in companies in various industry sectors as diverse as semiconductors, software, retailing and restaurants and others that may be specialists in only one technology.

While high technology investment makes up most of the venture investing in the U.S., and the venture industry gets a lot of attention for its high technology investments, venture capitalists also invest in companies such as construction, industrial products, business services, etc. There are several firms that have specialized in retail company investment and others that have a focus in investing only in "socially responsible" start-up endeavors.

Venture firms come in various sizes from small seed specialist firms of only a few million dollars under management to firms with over a billion dollars in invested capital around the world. The common denominator in all of these types of venture investing is that the venture capitalist is not a passive investor, but has an active and vested interest in guiding, leading and growing the companies they have invested in. They seek to add value through their experience in investing in tens and hundreds of companies.

Some venture firms are successful by creating synergies between the various companies they have invested in; for example one company that has a great software product, but does not have adequate distribution technology may be paired with another company or its management in the venture portfolio that has better distribution technology.

Length of Investment

Venture capitalists will help companies grow, but they eventually seek to exit the investment in three to seven years. An early stage investment make take seven to ten years to mature, while a later stage investment many only take a few years, so the appetite for the investment life cycle must be congruent with the limited partnerships' appetite for liquidity. The venture investment is neither a short term nor a liquid investment, but an investment that must be made with careful diligence and expertise.

Types of Firms

There are several types of venture capital firms, but most mainstream firms invest their capital through funds organized as limited partnerships in which the venture capital firm serves as the general partner. The most common type of venture firm is an independent venture firm that has no affiliations with any other financial institution. These are called "private independent firms". Venture firms may also be affiliates or subsidiaries of a commercial bank, investment bank or insurance company and make investments on behalf of outside investors or the parent firm's clients. Still other firms may be subsidiaries of non-financial, industrial corporations making investments on behalf of the parent itself. These latter firms are typically called "direct investors" or "corporate venture investors."

Other organizations may include government affiliated investment programs that help start up companies either through state, local or federal programs. One common vehicle is the Small Business Investment Company or SBIC program administered by the Small Business Administration, in which a venture capital firm may augment its own funds with federal funds and leverage its investment in qualified investee companies.

While the predominant form of organization is the limited partnership, in recent years the tax code has allowed the formation of either Limited Liability Partnerships, ("LLPs"), or Limited Liability Companies ("LLCs"), as alternative forms of organization. However, the limited partnership is still the predominant organizational form. The advantages and disadvantages of each has to do with liability, taxation issues and management responsibility.

The venture capital firm will organize its partnership as a pooled fund; that is, a fund made up of the general partner and the investors or limited partners. These funds are typically organized as fixed life partnerships, usually having a life of ten years. Each fund is capitalized by commitments of capital from the limited partners. Once the partnership has reached its target size, the partnership is closed to further investment from new investors or even existing investors so the fund has a fixed capital pool from which to make its investments.

Like a mutual fund company, a venture capital firm may have more than one fund in existence. A venture firm may raise another fund a few years after closing the first fund in order to continue to invest in companies and to provide more opportunities for existing and new investors. It is not uncommon to see a successful firm raise six or seven funds consecutively over the span of ten to fifteen years. Each fund is managed separately and has its own investors or limited partners and its own general partner. These funds' investment strategy may be similar to other funds in the firm. However, the firm may have one fund with a specific focus and another with a different focus and yet another with a broadly diversified portfolio. This depends on the strategy and focus of the venture firm itself.

Corporate Venturing

One form of investing that was popular in the 1980s and is again very popular is corporate venturing. This is usually called "direct investing" in portfolio companies by venture capital programs or subsidiaries of nonfinancial corporations. These investment vehicles seek to find qualified investment opportunities that are congruent with the parent company's strategic technology or that provide synergy or cost savings.

These corporate venturing programs may be loosely organized programs affiliated with existing business development programs or may be self-contained entities with a strategic charter and mission to make investments congruent with the parent's strategic mission. There are some venture firms that specialize in advising, consulting and managing a corporation's venturing program.

The typical distinction between corporate venturing and other types of venture investment vehicles is that corporate venturing is usually performed with corporate strategic objectives in mind while other venture investment vehicles typically have investment return or financial objectives as their primary goal. This may be a generalization as corporate venture programs are not immune to financial considerations, but the distinction can be made.

The other distinction of corporate venture programs is that they usually invest their parent's capital while other venture investment vehicles invest outside investors' capital.

Commitments and Fund Raising

The process that venture firms go through in seeking investment commitments from investors is typically called "fund raising." This should not be confused with the actual investment in investee or "portfolio" companies by the venture capital firms, which is also sometimes called "fund raising" in some circles. The commitments of capital are raised from the investors during the formation of the fund. A venture firm will set out prospecting for investors with a target fund size. It will distribute a prospectus to potential investors and may take from several weeks to several months to raise the requisite capital. The fund will seek commitments of capital from institutional investors, endowments, foundations and individuals who seek to invest part of their portfolio in opportunities with a higher risk factor and commensurate opportunity for higher returns.

Because of the risk, length of investment and illiquidity involved in venture investing, and because the minimum commitment requirements are so high, venture capital fund investing is generally out of reach for the average individual. The venture fund will have from a few to almost 100 limited partners depending on the target size of the fund. Once the firm has raised enough commitments, it will start making investments in portfolio companies.

Capital Calls

Making investments in portfolio companies requires the venture firm to start "calling" its limited partners commitments. The firm will collect or "call" the needed investment capital from the limited partner in a series of tranches commonly known as "capital calls". These capital calls from the limited partners to the venture fund are sometimes called "takedowns" or "paid-in capital." Some years ago, the venture firm would "call" this capital down in three equal installments over a three year period. More recently, venture firms have synchronized their funding cycles and call their capital on an as-needed basis for investment.

Illiquidity

Limited partners make these investments in venture funds knowing that the investment will be long-term. It may take several years before the first investments starts to return proceeds; in many cases the invested capital may be tied up in an investment for seven to ten years. Limited partners understand that this illiquidity must be factored into their investment decision.

Other Types of Funds

Since venture firms are private firms, there is typically no way to exit before the partnership totally matures or expires. In recent years, a new form of venture firm has evolved: so-called "secondary" partnerships that specialize in purchasing the portfolios of investee company investments of an existing venture firm. This type of partnership provides some liquidity for the original investors. These secondary partnerships, expecting a large return, invest in what they consider to be undervalued companies.

Advisors and Fund of Funds

Evaluating which funds to invest in is akin to choosing a good stock manager or mutual fund, except the decision to invest is a long-term commitment. This investment decision takes considerable investment knowledge and time on the part of the limited partner investor. The larger institutions have investments in excess of 100 different venture capital and buyout funds and continually invest in new funds as they are formed.

Some limited partner investors may have neither the resources nor the expertise to manage and invest in many funds and thus, may seek to delegate this decision to an investment advisor or so-called "gatekeeper". This advisor will pool the assets of its various clients and invest these proceeds as a limited partner into a venture or buyout fund currently raising capital. Alternatively, an investor may invest in a "fund of funds," which is a partnership organized to invest in other partnerships, thus providing the limited partner investor with added diversification and the ability to invest smaller amounts into a variety of funds.

Disbursements

The investment by venture funds into investee portfolio companies is called "disbursements". A company will receive capital in one or more rounds of financing. A venture firm may make these disbursements by itself or in many cases will co-invest in a company with other venture firms ("co-investment" or "syndication"). This syndication provides more capital resources for the investee company. Firms co-invest because the company investment is congruent with the investment strategies of various venture firms and each firm will bring some competitive advantage to the investment.

The venture firm will provide capital and management expertise and will usually also take a seat on the board of the company to ensure that the investment has the best chance of being successful. A portfolio company may receive one round, or in many cases, several rounds of venture financing in its life as needed. A venture firm may not invest all of its committed capital, but will reserve some capital for later investment in some of its successful companies with additional capital needs.

Exits

Depending on the investment focus and strategy of the venture firm, it will seek to exit the investment in the portfolio company within three to five years of the initial investment. While the initial public offering may be the most glamourous and heralded type of exit for the venture capitalist and owners of the company, most successful exits of venture investments occur through a merger or acquisition of the company by either the original founders or another company. Again, the expertise of the venture firm in successfully exiting its investment will dictate the success of the exit for themselves and the owner of the company.

IPO

The initial public offering is the most glamourous and visible type of exit for a venture investment. In recent years technology IPOs have been in the limelight during the IPO boom of the last six years. At public offering, the venture firm is considered an insider and will receive stock in the company, but the firm is regulated and restricted in how that stock can be sold or liquidated for several years. Once this stock is freely tradable, usually after about two years, the venture fund will distribute this stock or cash to its limited partner investor who may then manage the public stock as a regular stock holding or may liquidate it upon receipt. Over the last twenty-five years, almost 3000 companies financed by venture funds have gone public.

Mergers and Acquisitions

Mergers and acquisitions represent the most common type of successful exit for venture investments. In the case of a merger or acquisition, the venture firm will receive stock or cash from the acquiring company and the venture investor will distribute the proceeds from the sale to its limited partners.

Valuations

Like a mutual fund, each venture fund has a net asset value, or the value of an investor's holdings in that fund at any given time. However, unlike a mutual fund, this value is not determined through a public market transaction, but through a valuation of the underlying portfolio. Remember, the investment is illiquid and at any point, the partnership may have both private companies and the stock of public companies in its portfolio. These public stocks are usually subject to restrictions for a holding period and are thus subject to a liquidity discount in the portfolio valuation.

Each company is valued at an agreed-upon value between the venture firms when invested in by the venture fund or funds. In subsequent quarters, the venture investor will usually keep this valuation intact until a material event occurs to change the value. Venture investors try to conservatively value their investments using guidelines or standard industry practices and by terms outlined in the prospectus of the fund. The venture investor is usually conservative in the valuation of companies, but it is common to find that early stage funds may have an even more conservative valuation of their companies due to the long lives of their investments when compared to other funds with shorter investment cycles.

Management Fees

As an investment manager, the general partner will typically charge a management fee to cover the costs of managing the committed capital. The management fee will usually be paid quarterly for the life of the fund or it may be tapered or curtailed in the later stages of a fund's life. This is most often negotiated with investors upon formation of the fund in the terms and conditions of the investment.

Carried Interest

"Carried interest" is the term used to denote the profit split of proceeds to the general partner. This is the general partners' fee for carrying the management responsibility plus all the liability and for providing the needed expertise to successfully manage the investment. There are as many variations of this profit split both in the size and how it is calculated and accrued as there are firms.

Benefits and Advantages of Financing a Business with Venture Capital

Benefits

Venture capital investors may be the best or only plausible course for entrepreneurs who require a larger round of funding.

Venture capital allows investors to express their ideas about the future of the business. These individuals have a vested interest in the success of the business, because they would like to see a return on the investment. Therefore, the advice they give tends to be incisive and truthful.

Investors tend to have vast business experience, extensive networks and can mentor entrepreneurs in the art of growing their business.

Conclusion

Business owners must determine whether a business loan or venture capital will best suit their business needs. Small businesses are more qualified for business loans through lenders (and support from the small business loan administration program). There are several new government initiatives that will help small business owners retain loans. Some of the loan amounts are matched by the lenders or banks. If you desire to retain ownership of your business and the business idea has not fully developed, then a business loan is the better choice for you.

However, if the business plan is such that the company may involve complex software development and product development, then venture capital may be the best source of funding. Investors will review your business idea and determine the viability of the idea. Many of these ideas are carefully scrutinized. Therefore, business owners must be prepared to defend the idea. Business owners must be prepared to negotiate with investors throughout the duration of company.

Business owners must decide which option is more viable. Both funding methods have advantages and disadvantages depending on your business requirements, so often it simply comes down to deciding what disadvantages they would prefer while funding their idea.

CHAPTER FOUR

HOW FUNDING MINORITY BUSINESSES IS GOOD FOR AMERICA

Grants For Minorities - Free Money You Never Pay Back?

With the availability of grants for minorities, there are numerous opportunities for people of various backgrounds and ethnic groups to receive free money that never has to be paid back. These funds are available to qualified individuals and business owners as a way to help finance particular areas of interest. By submitting a minority grant application, individuals can find out if they are eligible to receive thousands of dollars in free grant money.

By searching the grant database, any individuals can view the hundreds of available grant funds. Minority federal funding in particular can provide those with particular backgrounds with money to buy a new home, get out of debt and cash for other personal expenses. Most notably are minority small business grants and grants for minority students.

The government and other private organizations strongly support minority businesses by providing free grant money to help individuals with small business start up costs. As much as $50,000 can be obtained to rent office space, purchase new equipment or furniture, and to hire employees. Minorities planning to start a home based Internet business can even qualify to receive free grant money to help source and purchase goods for sale.

Education grants for minorities are another hot area that receives significant support and attention. While college costs continue to rise, equal opportunity for minorities remains to be a priority when it comes to earning a college education. Minority funding for college students can help not only finance tuition costs every semester, but many programs can also help pay for other college expenses, such as books and student housing. Once obtained, many minority grants for college students can be received every semester.

While these cash funds are available to minorities at large, there are programs for specific ethnic groups as well, including:

- *Hispanic Grants*
- *African American Grants*
- *Asian American Grants*
- *American Indian Grants*
- *Disability Grants for Minorities*

As mentioned above, grants for minorities are not just limited to college students and small business owners. Government grants can help families with home improvement costs, pay for daycare, and even help with legal fees. Because grants are not loans, qualifying to receive these funds typically does not require a credit check, down payment or collateral. Find out if you qualify to receive free minority grant money right away.

Minority Grants For Small Businesses

The US Federal Government recognizes the issue of improving disadvantaged people's lives. Their constituents have voted congressmen and senators to power. Their primary election campaigns are based on the promise to minorities for their economic empowerment. t is these promises, which drive the politics of grant giving by Federal and local State governments.

Grants for Small Business:

A grant is a direct financial contribution made by certain organizations to the needy. It is made for very specific outcomes with no expectations of repayment. These grants are based on certain criteria and are designed to encourage entrepreneurs to start or expand their small business ventures. Millions of dollars in the form of small business grants are available for any minority group of Americans. They may be African Americans, Asian Americans, Hispanics, Indian Americans or any other minority.

Minority Grant Programs:

Government minority business grants are listed on all the government grants assistance programs. They allocate funds for lending to minority entrepreneurs, student business training, unemployed, community-based business opportunities, real-estate ventures and investment, research work and inventors, amongst others. A woman entrepreneur or an ethnic minority is entitled to funds specially earmarked for their business development.

Any entrepreneur seeking the fund for any type of business or any personal project must have a viable business plan. They should focus on how well their business would survive independent of these programs. Eventually, your aim should be to build a successful business. Have some sort of maturation plan in place to succeed without minority funds within three to five years. A lot of far-sightedness, hard work and perception of market need of your business are very important. If your business maturation plan is not in place, you are in a great risk of either business failure or being bought out. A good financial opportunity goes waste. So apply for these minority business grants and funding for a great opportunity to start your own venture and improve your social and financial status.

Types of Grants:

Ever since the Federal government has launched this minority grant for small businesses, the minority business has grown four times faster as overall US firms. Since 1992, the increase has been from 2.1 million to 2.8 million firms. These grants can be availed for:

o *For initial business start-up, you can avail up to one billion dollars from minority business grants.*

o *Grants in millions available for expanding the existing business*

o *Receive $9,000 in minority grants for free legal advice.*

o *Millions available for purchase of your first home*

o *Up to $75,000 available from minority grants to remodel your home*

o *Receive $6,000 in minority grants for college tuition.*

o *Receive free monthly grant finances for emergency assistance.*

o *Receive special assistance for woman entrepreneurship program. There are many more listed priorities to receive these grants.*

The federal government and local state government Active Affirmative Action has given a big opportunity to minor ethnic communities to start their small businesses. This will lead to their economic empowerment and social integration

What Are the Benefits of Minority Grants?

The government, as well as foundations all across the United States presents some grants that benefit the minority populations within various branches of businesses, work, and the research groups. Even though there are numerous minority grants that are being made available, for qualifying, you should meet eligibility requirements. They are different for people belonging to different origins. Let these requirements be studied one by one.

African Americans

African Americans have been experiencing a tremendous increase with respect to opportunities in terms of college grants since the last 10 years. They are inclusive of United Negro College Fund, Frederick Douglass Scholars Program, Mordecai Wyatt Johnson Program, The National Black Nurses Association, and The march of Dimes Nursing scholarships, The American Institute of Certified Public Accountants, and The American Psychological Association's minority fellowship program.

UNCF, i.e. The United Negro College Fund has been the most remarkable college grant for minorities so far. The year 1942 marks the foundation of UNCF. However, it had been in the year 1972 that the well-known phrase, "There is nothing more terrible to waste than the mind" got acknowledged all over the United States. This type of college grant for minority performs the task of funding around 3 dozens of historically African American universities and colleges.

Hispanic Minority Grants

Hispanic minority grants have been very few as compared to the other minorities. This deficit has been openly acknowledged by the US, thereby contributing around $15 m towards the start-up costs for developing Hispanic colleges and the universities. Apart from these funds, government has contributed around $70 m towards the already established colleges and the universities. United States might have gotten late start regarding the funding of this minority. However, dramatic enrollment has been observed with regards to their implementation.

Hispanic grants are inclusive of Hispanic Nurses association grants and scholarships, march of Dimes Nursing Scholarship Program, Scholarship for Disadvantaged students program, Nursing Education Loan Repayment program, The Hispanic Scholarship Fund Institute, Silicon valley Scholarship, and Jose Marti Challenge Grant.

Asian Minority Grants

He grants for minority that are given below correspond to one amongst the quickest minority assemblies in the US, i.e. the Asians. Luisa Mallari Fellowship has been the most powerful Asian grant for minority, that permits Asian students the chance of studying in the surrounding countries of theirs. There is a huge variety of grants for Asian minority, inclusive of Association for Asian Studies, Inc, Asian American Federation of New York, Asian American Journalists Association, Southeast Asian Studies Regional Exchange Program, and Luisa Mallari Fellowship.

Native American Minority Grants

In order to get qualified for Native American college grants, all you need to do is proof of CIB, i.e. Certificate of Indian blood of yours, along with belonging to any of the well-organized tribes. If you have been like majority of Native American descendants, there is a likelihood of you not having the proof, as most of the tribes who had their names changed didn't keep the documents. You won't be, in that case, eligible for the grants such as Indian Adult Education, Tribal Colleges Education Equity grants, Diabetes program, and many more.

CHAPTER FIVE

HOW VC'S COULD AND SHOULD MAKE A DIFFERENCE

What Venture Capitalists Want to make Difference

We all have a vision of the Venture Capitalist. Often times that vision is a mistaken one of something akin to the Marlboro Man. The truth is there are as many types of funding sources for entrepreneurs and businesses as there are makes, models, and colors of vehicles on the roads. This diversity precludes a single brush stroke describing them all.

Just as each of us has developed likes and dislikes from experience, the same can be said of VC's. Not all desire equity positions in your undertaking either. Some deliberately eschew the opportunity. Others demand the voice and control an equity position provides.

However, there are concerns common to all lenders / investors. When seeking funding for a business endeavor, it helps to immerse yourself in the mindset of the VC. Take a marketing approach. Your story needs to be compelling, your business plan complete. Think like they do. Ask yourself, what is in it for them? They certainly will ask that question, repeatedly. What do they really want and need from an entrepreneur?

Who are You?

Bankers lend funds provided by their depositors. FDIC requirements dictate the borrower hold commensurate collateral securing the principal. Entrepreneurial endeavors seldom possess such hard assets; creating the need for riskier and more expensive venture capital. Other far more nebulous 'assets' of the borrower becomes highly important. Who makes up your management team? Is this Act II or better for you and them? What is their background and education? What direct experiences have they in this industry? A carpenter opening his first restaurant probably will not endear much support. At least one VC claims not to invest in good ideas at all, rather it invests in good people. Competent management is essential.

What is Your Idea?

So, what is this great idea of yours? What are its advantages, along with its inherent disadvantages? Expecting VC's to sign confidentiality agreements before your unveiling proves you are not ready for classic venture capital. Be prepared to tell them everything. You are asking for their money, open up and provide them the information they need. Trust needs to be mutual.

Who is Your Customer and why will they buy Your Product?

Seldom is a product so new, so different, and so advantageous that people immediately abandon the old reliable in favor of it. If your offer truly is new, you face an adoption curve. The PC, cell phones, and DVD's each took time to penetrate the market despite their advantages. How do your intended customers satisfy current needs? What are their alternatives to you? Your competitors: what are their strengths and weaknesses? Espousing you have no competition suggests you are unrealistic. What is the single compelling reason for customers to switch to you?

Amazon was not the first to attempt internet sales. But they were the first major success. They kept a focus on books and asserted their advantage, 30% off.

How much of your product will they buy?

Pie in the sky sales estimates will kill any chance you have of securing capital. Where do your numbers come from? What assumptions have you made? What impact will external forces, such as a sputtering economy or an interest rate increase have, if any?

To protect investors, some VC's actually cut sales estimates in half gauging the effect on the financials. They presume estimates are influenced both by hope and dreams. What will create customer loyalty? Everybody claims to offer high product quality, great service, and the lowest pricing. You have to do better than that, if you want the money.

Is your offering a once in a lifetime purchase, or a consumable requiring repeat purchases?

PC printers are sold at rock bottom prices to gain entry to repeat ink cartridge sales. Design deliberately inhibits competitive cartridge pricing. This is where their continuing profits are made. What's your hook?

How will you put the money to work?

What assets will you purchase with the cash provided? How will these resources be employed? How does each invested dollar affect sales? This is probably the biggest mistake made approaching a VC: failing to make a convincing case the money provided will generate cash, now! Unlike some wines that gain value lounging around, venture capitalists do not want their money aging, particularly in your account, they want it working. Nothing motivates them more than the "ker-ching" of the cash register. Demonstrate specifically how the cash will go to work now, and you are well on your way. If funding is required for further product research and development, your enterprise is probably not ready for classic venture capital.

When is Payday?

How long do you need the funds? When is the payoff? How big will it be? What is the essence of your offer to these capitalists? Do your forecasted statements include payments to them? Displaying pro formas absent of such provisions will do little to create a warm cozy feeling in a venture capitalist's heart. Suggesting that value will one day be obvious for a buyout is of little comfort.

The exit strategy for the investor has to be planned just as well as the entry. Without a clear exit strategy, your plan is incomplete. Would you buy a half cooked egg, or half a pair of pants? Without a complete business plan, you're probably wasting your time and theirs.

Choosing to fund only a very small portion of the total number of proposals they evaluate proves a lot of work needs to be done by entrepreneurs on their presentation skills. Venture capitalists are looking to earn profits. Show them how you can accomplish this for the both of you, and you will have your money.

Four Steps Towards Attracting Venture Capital Investments

Most startup companies don't have much capital to begin with and struggle to remain open. They turn to outside investor support until they can achieve profitability. If you are the owner of a small business, then you know that getting your company funding is one of the most difficult business challenge you can face.

Seeking this venture capital is an increasingly growing trend fueled by a combination of several factors, such as: improvement in the IPO market, abundant entrepreneurial talent, promising new technologies, and government policies favoring venture capital formation. It's no wonder why venture investors continue to launch and support the development of so many new technologies and business concepts.

Venture capital investments give you and your company the resources it needs to grow to it's full potential since it is used for a variety of things. For example, you can invest in top notch talent, new machinery, manual laborers or you may need to invest in research or new technology. To help put you on the track towards securing venture capital, here are four steps to attract the attention of venture capital investors:

➢ *One of the most important steps is to network*. It is one of the first steps in attracting that elusive venture capital. Actually business networking is an important tool for your business all around. The idea behind networking is get the the name of your company out there in the minds of people in the industry and create some buzz around your business idea. If you get the change collect business cards as a way of beginning a path towards contacts.

➢ *You are going to need an experienced team of business partners behind you*. One of the things venture capitalists look at it is how well of a structured organization of a company you have and how loyal your co-workers are. Build a diverse team of great minds and sell its credentials to attract some venture capital. TA great group of team members helps to further develop that all crucial buzz which leads to venture capital investment.

➢ *Put together a professional presentation to sell your company's goal and ideas*. A smooth, sophisticated presentation should answers all possible questions clearly and avoids any challenges with solutions. This should bring your venture capitalist talks to the next step. Give your solid presentation to as many business associates as you can. Always continue to modify it so that it reaches the level of satisfaction it needs.

> ➤ *Media coverage brings nothing but benefits.* Anytime you can to put yourself on TV or get your name in the newspaper, take it. For example, if your company is in the tech-field or involves the internet, contact review sites and magazines. Writing press releases and submitting them to local newspapers is a great way to catch the eye or a possible venture capital firm

CHAPTER SIX

THE CASE FOR DARK KNIGHT CAPITAL VENTURES

Being a Capital Venture Investor

There are two types of people in the world. These are the rich who have money and those that don't. When the person has money, there will be no problems going on a shopping spree in New York or hop on board a plane to see paradise in the Bahamas. The average Joe can also do that but will have to same that amount over a few months or even years.

If the rich individual doesn't do anything to preserve the wealth, this will soon disappear. This is the reason that being a venture capital investor seems to be a good idea.

A venture capital investor is an individual who would like to help fund an entrepreneur. There are two kinds namely the person who will wait to receive such a proposal while the other is out there hoping to see something interesting.

In the end, the venture capital investor will be reviewing the business plan to make sure it is sound and also meet the entrepreneur in person to clarify some issues. There are some people who might take advantage of the individual so a background check will be done even before the meeting takes place.

The venture capital investor who is well aware of the trends for example in the information technology will not want to do business in a field that is unknown to that individual.

This means the person will only gamble on a high-risk investment in the preferred comfort zone. This approach is advantageous to the entrepreneur because the years of experience in that field can be useful in the partnership.

What does a capital venture investor get from all of this? In exchange for the money being shelled by the individual, there are also a certain number of shares that will be given to get a seat among the board of directors.

This will ensure that the investor can play an active role in the direction of the business to be able to safeguard the money that was invested into the project.

As the company grows, the money invested by the investor will be returned and the profits will be shared increasing the current wealth of the person.

Being a venture capitalist is a win-win situation for the individual and the entrepreneur. After all, two heads are better than one in making the day-to-day decisions so the company will become profitable in the long run.

At Dark Knight Capital Ventures:

We help entrepreneurs and venture capital fund managers turn promising ideas into market-defining and market-leading businesses. We are committed to spreading the Dark Knight Capital Ventures through our investment activity as well as in the other ways we engage with the entrepreneurial ecosystem.

We're mutifaceted entrepreneurs, financial analysts, tech geeks, and investors—and we're passionate about helping achieve TRUE Diversity. We seek to introduce more women, minorities, and underserved founders into the Market!

Founded by Jason M. Fields, after years of seeing emerging founders with great products, services, and innovative ideas get rejected and leave his hometown, Jason decided that enough was enough, "If we are truy going to help our community, we must foster, believe, and support emerging market founders and assist them with leaving their mark in history.

Jason M. Fields, CFEI (Certified Financial Education Instructor). The founder of Dark Knight Capital Ventures, he holds a BS Degree in Business Management- Cardinal Stritch

University. Jason is the Founder and President of GlobalEx, LLC Holdings. He is also the Co-Founder and Partner of DiversifyForex, a Foreign Currency, Stock, and Binary Options Investment Education Firm.

In 2005, Jason became the first African-American man to be elected to the Wisconsin State Assembly 11th District.

He is a published author having written two books. He is currently working on his CHP (Certified Hedge Fund Professional) designation.

Jason started his career in the financial services sector where he helped actively manage over $100 million in assets. His experience includes bonds, equities, derivatives, insurance and residential and commercial loans.

Regardless of the size of our initial investment, the size and structure of our funds allow us to continue to fund portfolio companies through their entire financing lifecycles. In addition, our venture capital fund investments give us insight and access to a large number of venture-backed companies at varying stages while extending the reach of our overall network.

In addition to providing capital, we leverage our experience in starting and growing companies, our expertise in the technology industry, and our network of relationships to help outstanding entrepreneurs and venture capital fund managers turn great ideas into great companies.

About Venture Capital Investors

While evaluating the profitability of venture capital investment proposals under the capital budgeting techniques such as Net Present Value (NPV) and Internal Rate of return are used. It should be noted here that these sophisticated methods use the "cost of capital" as the criterion to accept or reject an investment proposal.

Under the NPV method, the cost of capital is used to discount the future cash flows, whereas under the Internal Rate of return method, the cost of capital is compared with the calculated Internal rate of return in order to determine the efficacy of the capital investment proposals.

The minimum required rate of return that a firm must earn on its investments in order to keep the present wealth of the shareholders unchanged or keep the market value of the firm's equity shares is referred to as "cost of capital". In the context of evaluating the investment projects, cost of capital refers to the discount rate used for evaluating the desirability of the investment proposals.

Cost of capital plays a crucial role in the sphere of capital budgeting decisions. It serves as an important basis for financial appraisal of new capital investment proposals. For instance, the cost of capital is compared with the discounted rate of return to determine whether the proposed project satisfies one of the minimum acceptable standards. The expected rate of returns on a project must be greater than the cost of capital.

If the cost of capital of a firm is known, it is possible to make a fair estimation of the amount of risks that is involved in the company's investment projects. For instance, if a firm were required to pay more than the market rate of interest in order to procure funds from the investors, this would show investors that the earnings rate of the firm is moderate or less and that the firm has limited opportunities to develop in future.

Thank you again for downloading this book!

I hope this book was able to help you to (fill in the blank).

The next step is to (fill in the blank).

Finally, if you enjoyed this book, then I'd like to ask you for a favor, would you be kind enough to leave a review for this book on Amazon? It'd be greatly appreciated!

Click here to leave a review for this book on Amazon!

Thank you and good luck!

ONE LAST THING...

If you enjoyed this book or found it useful I'd be very grateful if you'd post a short review on Amazon. Your support really does make a difference and I read all the reviews personally so I can get your feedback and make this book even better.

If you'd like to leave a review then all you need to do is click the review link on this book's page on Amazon here.

Thanks again for your support!

Printed in the United States
By Bookmasters